Forever to an Underwood Typewriter

Doug D'Elia

Acknowledgements

The author wishes to thank the editors of the following publications:

"Crossing Midnight" appears in Wayfarer (March, 2014)

"Cottage Envy" appears in Poetry Jumps Off the Self (Contest winner – this poem appears on maple syrup bottles at select outlets in Wisconsin and Vermont, 2014)

"The Aviaries of God" appears in Bette Noir (Issue 17, 2014)

"Dead Witches in Cold Well Water" appears in H_ngM_n Press (Summer, 2014)

"Little Warning" appears in Central Florida Anthology (2015)

"Medical Horses" appears in Kind of a Hurricane Press (Spring 2015) and Storm Cycle, Best of Kind of a Hurricane Anthology (2015)

Content

Crossing Midnight

Imagine for a moment that your
vision is limited to just one hour of each day.
Which hour would you choose?

Would you choose to see in the hour after waking?
Beginning each day with the joy of your lover's
smile or the faces of your children.

Would you choose to stroll along the beach?
Watching the morning mist swirl above the water
like a thousand wind blown wedding veils?

Would you hike into the woods?
To linger among lush plant and leaf,
a palette-world painted in shades of green.

Would you choose midday?
To watch clouds disguised as dragons
and teapots, move across a blue sky.

Would you wait for dusk?
When the sun turns from yellow to red
as it shimmies below the horizon?

Would you choose the pitch of night?
Reclining under the moonlight with you lover,
her eyes as bright as a constellation. Or

would you choose the hour that crosses midnight?
When you say a gratitude for the day past
and express your hope for the day ahead,

as she looks at you as if you are magic,
thankful to hear your voice in the one hour
that she has chosen to hear.

Gratitude Kites

It's difficult to lose a wife
        of so few years,
to make meaning of it beyond,
        It was her time.
Her death was even more difficult for my
        5-year-old daughter.
I recited her the customary metaphors,
        She's gone to heaven.
She's with God and the angels.
        She'll be watching over us.
She'll be waiting for us when we arrive.

She was quiet and gloomy, until one day
        she saw kids flying kites
and she had her wonderful idea.
        To write notes to her mother
on the end of a kite, and to fly it high in the sky,
        then release it to heaven.
I suggested she express her gratitude
        for their time together,
and the things that made her laugh
        and smile.
And we bought a bright yellow kite
        and decorated it
with red hearts and notes, and letting it go,
        sent it towards heaven
watching it became a speck that then
        melted from sight.
It was wonderful to see her so happy and she asked
        if we could send a kite up each year
on the date of her mother's passing, and

we agreed we would.

So we sent a kite to heaven the next year and
    the year after that,
and the third year, in sadness and despair,
    I drew hearts on the kite and
attached a note thanking my daughter
    for her imagination and creativity.
and sent the kite adrift in the direction
    of heaven
where Mother and daughter hovered
    hand-in-hand. Waiting.

A Dead Fish at the Bottom of My Soup Bowl

When I was not feeling well,
Grandma would warm chicken broth
and carefully pour it into
a porcelain bowl a friend
had brought her from China.
The bowl had been carefully
hand painted with a colorful koi fish
at the bottom, and the China bowl
was only taken from the cupboard
on special occasions,

Grandma told me that when I
finished my soup there would
be a surprise at the bottom
of the bowl, which brought to mind
the prizes that I had pulled
from a box of Cracker Jack's,
a toy soldier or a small whistle,
some plastic token that would hold
my attention for a few minutes.

My predicament was that through
the rust colored broth, I could already
see the colorful koi fish laying still
at the bottom of the bowl,
but I didn't have the heart to tell
Grandma that her surprise, the fish,
had already died. So I told her
I was too sick to eat, and I was.
The sight of that dead fish in my soup
made me nauseous. I mean what kind

of surprise is that anyway, a fish at the
bottom of your soup bowl?
I've never forgotten that afternoon
with Grandma, and the dead fish in my bowl.
It was certainly better than anything
I could have pulled out of a Cracker Jack box.

China's Bureau of Tourism

The two boys digging with plastic
shovels on the beach at Cape Cod
said they were digging a hole to
    China.

And I hear that if you really put your back
into it on the beaches of Rio in Brazil
you pop-up in a small village outside
    Beijing.

And evidently if you dig deep enough
on Yalong Beach at the South China Sea
you'll arrive somewhere around
    Xinjiang

in the northern province of Mongolia.
The Bureau's official brochure promises
that the fortunate arrive along the
    Yangtze River

at night when the moon is enuf,
and campfires are visible
in the distant mountains of
    Tibet,

at a place where wise poets spend the night
writing haiku, inspired by the moon,
just returned from a long night in
    Shanghai.

Cottage Envy

You shouldn't envy me, really.
It's merely time at the cottage.
Spent in solitude, enjoying
magnificent trees through
the swirling mist off the lake.
You can do the same
at home in a hot steamy bath,
with a house plant.
So don't envy me. Besides
I'm bringing you maple syrup.

Dead Witches in Cold Well Water

Must be the season of the witch.
Must be the season of shape shifters,
mischievously biting and pinching.

Must be the season to hear the
rattle of wagon wheels and the snorting
of nags trudging under the weight of
condemned witches, towards cold Gallows Hill,
where crows with shiny pitch black feathers
pass time cackling from the safety of tree limbs.

Must be the season to parade our children
town to town, cruelly using them like a divining rod
to point out the accused guilty of nothing more than
enjoying a midnight walk under the magic of
stars and the glow of a full moon.

Must be hanging season when our young children
are obliged to attend public displays of the macabre
to deter immoral impulses. The season to watch
bodies spinning from creaky scaffolds, their faces
turning the color of ripe eggplant as their feet
search frantically for higher ground.

Must be the season to live in fear of clergy
that gather to fast and pray for the
strength and resolve to pry confessions
from innocent children, to excommunicate,
to exorcise demons out of the carnal body
as if they were the Messiah.
Must be the season to lower pagans

into the dark abyss of the shaft, condemned
to sit in cold well water until night's shadow
covers the hole and no one comes to draw water.

Little Warning

When I was a boy
I was bitten by
a German Shepherd.

He came up fast
and silent. I heard his
growl only seconds

before he bit into me.
It was like that for my
friend Danny, too.

He only heard the
screech of tires just
before the car hit him.

And my cousin Ray
heard the click of the landmine,
that took off both his legs,

having only a brief second
to think, Oh, no!
I wonder how the world ends?

Will there be a growl, a bite,
or a click of a warning.
Just enough time to give thanks

or contemplate a comforting thought,
I'm on my way home now God.
Or maybe we don't get that

little warning. Maybe our souls
are just heaved – in one big swoosh -
back out among the stars.

On Sleepless Roads the Sleepless Go

On sleepless roads the sleepless go
over hill and down dale to green
pastures

to lay quietly on fresh grass
among dusty-mouthed
shepherds

weary single-filers
insomniac travelers
who dream of vagrants walking

on sleepless roads where
restless loners keep company
with idle shadow lovers

pebble kickers and scratch pad
writers that read novellas
about drifters on dusty roads

just passing through with cigarette
stained discolored fingers
and coffee-colored eyes

a handful of gimme and a mouth
full of much obliged
an ex-pat with an alias and false

credentials for every border crossing
shadow boxing shape shifters
lingering sad-eyed ghosts

as confident as an insomniac's dream
taking shelter from the storm
on Sleepless Roads the Sleepless Go

Shaman Whistle Woman

The first time I saw her
she scared the hell out of me,
reeds spouting from her neck
like children's flutes.

Scraggly root-grass hair
braided with sea glass and beads
curled around her arms like weeds,
rattled down each arm to her wrist.

Her hypnotic breasts slightly noticeable
under plates of copper and hawk feathers,
that dangle over a meadow skirt fashioned
from colorful butterflies and beetles.

As she drew closer I smelt the medicinal
herbs that she had dried and baked
in nature's forest kiln, and now
wears in a pouch around her neck.

And as she approached, she emitted
an eerie rhythmic, soothing,
low-spark hum, a vibration dart
that rendered me helpless, as she leaned

towards me a reed extended from her neck
to my lips. I hesitated as a fussy infant
turns from the nipple before
it realizes it is about to be nourished.

Play she whispered in my ear, make music with me.

And I wafted on her neck creating a whistling
sound that excited the jungle, driving the birds
from their nests, and sending monkeys

to the protection of the river.
The sound of an arrow rushing through the air,
on target, the thud and deep exhale
of the soul leaving the body.

The Aviaries of God

The presence of creatures
with wings is terrifying.
It shouldn't be, but it is.

A choir of them cackling
in strange, noisy, high-shrilled
dialects, like a murder of ravens.

Their dark feathery wings attached
to perfect bodies in grotesque
strangeness.

Mops of black Iroquois hair
slicked back in the shape
of burial shrouds.

Preparing to come to Earth
in disguise, to entertain unaware,
as if no one would notice.

Banana Boat Dancers

I was thinking about the deadly black tarantulas
that hide under bunches of bananas on the boat
Day-O,

and the muscular suntanned Tally Man
who handles the tall stacks

without the reassurance of protective gloves -
six foot, seven foot, eight foot bunch.

It's little wonder that banana-boat-men,
drink rum and sing all day,

pleased as pirates, sallying their yellow-jacketed
dance partners from bow to stern,

while under banana leaves, jealous high-stepping
rumba-loving tarantulas, decked-out in fur coats,

crowd the dance floor, jerking to and fro,
in the heat of the Caribbean sun.

At days end, the welcome sight of a Havana moon,
as exhausted dancers, one and all, head for home.

Day-O, Day-O.

Antarctic Summer

The metal hinges
of the wooden coffin
rattle when it slams shut,

and the swing of the watchman's
hammer against rusty nails
rains splinters and sawdust

into the darkness of the crypt
where Nosferatu hides
from six months of sunlight,

resting his misshapen head
on ancient white pillows,
embroidered with scarlet trim

that match his bloodshot eyes.
And as the earth spins on its axis
Nosferatu idly passes the time,

cleaning and sharpening his teeth
with his long reptilian tongue,
waiting for an orchestra of crickets

and the howling of wolves
to announce the renewal of his season,
Hark, the fallen angels sing.

The moon, returning from vacation
in the True North of the deep south,
enuf with expectation.

Idioms

I've got all my ducks in a row,
a undertaking more difficult
than previously assumed.

Yet some still downgrade
ducks in a row listing it after
putting all your eggs in one basket,

an errand in which I have little interest.
I would put *eggs in one basket* in the same
category as *getting a handle* on something,

which I'd like to point out, if you haven't
already noticed, isn't anymore original
than *getting a grip*.

It's certainly nothing like
barking up the wrong tree
which I always enjoy watching,

but would never consider.
If I'm going to risk embarrassment,
biting off more than I can chew

is well worth mastering
especially where
sweets are involved,

but isn't having a mouth full of anything
you can't chew the same as
having your cake and eating it too?

Peacock Eyes

If you didn't see her
beneath me
you might think I was
practicing yoga
under the shade of a maple.
My lower body,
trembling, unable to hold
the pose,
my chest and head
arching skyward.

While the resident prized
peacock patrols the yard,
ground-feeding,
pretending not to care,
mocking my involuntary groans,
fanning its tail feathers to reveal
hundreds of blue, green
and gold eyes, each
staring in my direction,
Really, professor. Really?

The condescending fool
of a foul, flaunting the same
grand, iridescent train he
waves to entice his harem,
cock sure,

as I lower myself to her again,
my face contorted, staring not into
her eyes but his, imagining plucking
the testy little peacock naked.

Being Ali

When you said you were Cassius Clay
and you were The Greatest we asked you,
What kind of name is Cassius?

When you said your name was
Muhammad Ali we asked you,
What is wrong with the name Cassius Clay?

When you said Malcolm X was your mentor
and you were a convert to the Nation of Islam
we asked you, Why have you forsaken Christianity?

When you said you didn't have a quarrel
with the Vietcong. We said you were a
draft dodger. We said you should be like Elvis.

When you were convicted, stripped of your
boxing belt and banned from the ring for five years,
we said you got what you deserve.

Then we realized you were right about
religious freedom and racial injustice,
you were even right about Vietnam.

We watched you earn back your crown.
We gave you awards and honorary degrees.
We invited you, a Muslim, to light the Olympic torch.

We respected that you took a stand for that
which you believed. That you lived your life
with passions and conviction.

We no longer needed you to be like Elvis,
We appreciated that that you were being Ali.
Muhammad Ali. The great Muhammad Ali.

Chinese Poets

Chinese poets
spend far too much time
looking up at the moon,

obsessively pondering
phases of waxing and waning,
gibbons and crescents.

Du Fu looked up.
Wang Wei looked up.
Li Po, it is reported,

drowned when he leaned over his boat
attempting to grasp the moon
reflected in the lake.

That's how I imagined the
Chinese poets, compelled under the
spell of tradition, to look up.

Until I learned about Yue Lao
The Old Man On The Moon who,
it is reported, holds the power to grant wishes.

And so I climbed to the mountain summit,
to the encampment where lovers come to petition
wedding blessings. And I danced with the

spirits of Du Fu, Wang Wei, and Li Po.
I danced around the campfire drinking wine
in the scent of a cinnamon tree.

And every month when the moon enuf,
at the summit of the mountain I make a wish
and looking up toss pennies at the moon.

Hey, Jack Kerouac

Hey, Jack Kerouac, rucksack over your shoulder,
hopping a westbound train from the Orange
Blossom Trail freight yards to Brownsville,
where a leather-skinned old man in a rusty Chevy
truck drives you across the border, and takes you
as far as you are going.
That's the way to live!

Hitching down the Mexican coast like some ex-pat.
Ready for adventure. Stopping to swim in Tampico
Bay. The salt water sticking to your body like salt on
the rim of a cold margarita. In your swim shorts
drinking cerveza, barefooted, wild haired, singing,
swinging, lying, spitting, jumping, running,
that's the way to live!

Slugging down shots of tequila on the roof of a de-
crepit hotel under a starry Mayan sky, in trace,
channeling 242 choruses of Mexico City Blues.
Punching at typewriter keys like a wild-eyed under-
dog prize fighter, spent and delirious, who senses
the decisive knockout.
That's the way to live!

Writing under the heat of a serape, tequila, and
peyote conjuring up hallucinations of senoritas,
singing cantatas, hell-bent on swinging from roof to
roof on frayed ropes. Mexican magi bearing the gift
of words translated from the Aztec language. That's
the way to live, Jack Kerouac.
That's the way to live!

If I Should Pass You On The Way Down

I marvel at the sight of you.
A perfect combination of
strength and fragility.

Your pedals rising up through
a narrow crack in the cement sidewalk,
so far from Earth's green fields that

Mother Nature herself must have brought
you forth as a reminder that she
cannot be suppressed by dystopian vision.

That every garden starts with a seed that
crawls wispy from the womb of Mother Earth,
is breast fed on fresh air and sunlight,

watered with love and gratitude,
caressed by the wind, and brought-up on
childlike parables that hearten

us to push upwards, to bend
towards the light regardless.
You are inspiration, little one.

If I could but have your spirit!
Instead I hesitant at every crack,
fearful of falling into darkness.

Therefore, I propose a partnership
that I become co-caretaker of the garden.
I will till, plant, and nature,

and should I slip or fall into a crack and
if I should pass you on the way down,
extend unto to me your strongest root

that I may hold firm and pull myself up through
narrow shaft, gripping the reins of hope
and riding bravely upon a ray of golden sunlight.

Lynching Cats

They probably shouldn't be allowed
to watch any more Saturday morning westerns,
I'm talking about the kids that patrol
the back allies of Holyoke.

Last night a posse of them exercised
their own brand of vigilante justice
by tracking down a stray alley cat,
tying one end of a rope around its neck
and the other around a second-floor
railing then tossing it off the porch.

This morning we all saw its lifeless body,
eyes popping, mouth distorted, dangling from
the porch. It scared the hell out of everyone
who lived in the apartment block, especially Marie,
the French-Canadian woman who lives
on the second floor with her lilac-grey Siamese
cat Marcel, who she hurried away from the window.

A lynching is a shocking sight, and everyone
kept their distance until Edgar, the butcher,
cut down the cat with a clever and tossed it
into the incinerator chute. The back alley
was quickly restored to normal, the ragman
made his rounds, as did the iceman, the milkman,
and the paperboy – both morning and evening
deliveries. I played stickball with friends. Over our
heads, the grey soot spewed from the incinerator's
chimney. In the winter it resembled snow, but in
summer it was volcanic ash.

Marie, that Frenchy Papou, was back at the window, cradling Marcel in her arms. He purred smugly from under the safety of Marie's perfumed breasts, his tiny Christmas bell jingling from his elongated neck.

The Chinese Laundry

The only Chinese person I had ever seen
was the television detective Charlie Chan,
but even without the white suit and top hat,
long braids or Fu Manchu beard,
I could tell that he was Chinese.

He bowed slightly when collecting
Dad's laundry claim check, and then scanned
the shelf of plain brown paper bundles
that were secured with string and arranged
alphabetically until he found our last name.

To my surprise, he calculated the cost of the
transaction on an abacus, by moving beads up,
down and across with deft confidence. It was a
system of counting that I had never encountered
and I wondered why I hadn't been introduced to the
bead game in school.

The Chinese man looked at me and bowed
and Dad introduced me,
This is my son, Douglas.
The man from China smiled,
Ah, number one son.
He reached under the counter
and gave me a piece of candy wrapped in paper
with Chinese writing.

Everything about this Saturday morning was neat.
As I crossed the street holding Dad's hand
I felt like an explorer just returned from the Orient,

wondering what other wonders awaited my discovery. One day, I promised myself, I would take my number one son to the Chinese laundry.

The Lady Who Writes Poems on Chinese Menus

She was a late arrival to Poetry Night,
because she relied on the unreliable city bus.
So she quietly slipped into the chair by the door
and listened intently to other poets read their work.

And when it was her turn, her hand circled the
inside of her oversized handbag until she found
what she was looking for, a Chinese restaurant
menu, a bilingual edition with English written in
one column and Mandarin across from it, duck
sauce stained each column indiscriminately.

The poets eyes darted across the menu,
from marker to marker, as if she
were studying a treasure map for the location
of a poem she had carefully hidden between prices
and spicy pepper warnings.

When she found the trail of what she had written,
she began to read, slowly turning the menu at
different angles, following her handwriting around
General Tso's Chicken and the Cantonese Sweet and
Sour Egg Rolls.

And when she finished reading her poem,
she put the menu back in her bag and walked
to the bus stop where she used her mini
leave a comment, pencil to begin her edits.

Wandering Aengus

It had become a glimmering girl
With apple blossom in her hair
Who called me by my name and ran
And faded through the brightening air.

W.B Yates
Song of the Wandering Aengus

Aengus, that troubled soul.
Wandering the knolls and bogs
of Ireland looking for that
vision of beauty with apple blossoms
in her hair who appeared to him in a dream,
and offered her love-song heart.

Aengus, a fire in his head,
chasing one bad lead after another,
a year in passing, mad with desire
turning, in desperation to the Oracle,
whose prophecy told him her name is
whispered in the caves of Newgrange.

Aengus running faster than Saint Peter
to the tomb of Jesus, through hollow lands,
and hilly lands, to the mouth of the cave
where no angel sat in waiting to spread
the Good News, only a bewildered

Aengus staring at 100 beautiful women
chained in pairs along a stone wall,
his ears swelling from the screeching

of his name, Aengus! Pick me. Pick me!
I'm the woman of your dreams!

The Rattle of the Tin Cup

Douglas, go give your
nickel to that bum.
Mom to author
1951

I like the sound of a nickel
rattling around in my tin cup.
I like the sound a quarter
makes better, but as they say,
beggars can't be choosy.

It's been slow at the bus station,
but my season is coming;
Thanksgiving and Christmas
right around the corner.
Today, it's not quite cold enough
for people to care, but I shiver anyway.

I put a few pennies in my cup,
and when people approach
I rattle it good, shake it
like a tambourine to
attract attention to myself.
It's tells them I exist.

A mom with her young son approach
so I rattle the cup. She fishes around
in her purse, but doesn't catch anything.
I hear her tell the boy,
Go give the nickel I gave you to that bum.
That's what they call me, Bum.

It doesn't mean I'm a bad person,
I'm just down on my luck.

The boy glances over at me,
but doesn't move until he is nudged.
With his head down he walks over to me
with his nickel held tightly in his palm.
I can tell that he has yet to grasp the virtue
of charity. I want to tell him it's ok,
that I won't use his nickel
to buy booze or cigarettes.
This time I'll buy a cup of coffee,
maybe some soup, or a sandwich.
Without looking at me, he drops the nickel
into my cup where it bounces off a few pennies
and a bus token. The boy, now carrying nothing
but a handful of sadness, scuffles back to his
mother side and together they board the
big smelly red bus on steps made for adults.
He sits in the front of the bus in a window seat.
His head lowered, his lips pouting.
I rattle the cup. I want to get his attention.
I want to tell him it's all right.
I want to tell him he'll have other nickels.
I want to tell him that sometimes
you're given a nickel and sometimes
it's taken away. Life is funny like that.
Just be sure to always keep a few pennies
in your cup, and rattle it loud when
people approach or when you need
to remind yourself you exist.

Sorry You Missed Sinatra

Father spent his honeymoon
at Niagara Falls, on the U.S. side.
He remembers the roar of the
water crashing against the rocks
and the spray of rainbows
shimmering in the mist.

Mother said she spent her honeymoon
at the Paramount Theatre in New York City.
She remembers the Benny Goodman
orchestra playing with Frank Sinatra!

The first time I heard these unalike accounts
I wondered how my was father,
the immigrant boy from Naples, Italy,
didn't remember seeing Frank Sinatra
on his honeymoon. Or why my mother
didn't remember the breath-taking
beauty and romantic appeal of Niagara Falls.

Over the years, the subject came up
more often than you might imagine.
It didn't matter to me, either way,
who was right or wrong. The exchange
was always light-hearted and in some
odd way I think it was a means of
intimate communication between them.

Mother would chide him
you never had much of a memory.
Dad, would counter, I should know

where I spent my honeymoon, I was there!
And then mom's predictable response,
Then you were with someone else,
because I was at the Paramount with Frank Sinatra.

Both my parents lived to see 90 years,
clinging to separate memories of their
honeymoon until the day they died.
I do miss hearing the lively banter,
though I did dream recently that the discussion
had changed to who had died first.
Dad was clinging to his well-worn line,
You died first, I should know I was there.
Mother interrupting, Can't you be quiet,
I'm trying to listen to old green-eyes.
Dad blurting out, Sinatra has blue eyes!
What do you know? She screamed.
You were at Niagara Falls!
Even the angels sighed.

The 12-year-old Mexican Poet Boy

Juan de Vargas, the 12-year-old poet boy, was a
guest at the Governor's

       inauguration.

The Governor loves poetry, especially that written
by Mexican

       poets.

Among the Governor's best chocolate makers is a
woman who once

       lived

in the remote mountain village with the remarkable
12-year-old poet

       boy.

So a message was sent summoning Juan to read at
the Governor's

       festivities.

The night before the inauguration the inhabitants of
the village, dressed in

       colorful

serapes and sturdy scandals made from tree bark,

set out to

walk

all night along the 30 mile path that connects the
Governor's town to the

village

to hear the boy read the poem he had written for
the

Governor.

The village people arrived at daylight and sat quiet-
ly at the back of the Governor's

grounds

awaiting the poet boy's reading of the poem he had
written for the

Governor.

And when Juan had read his poem the village peo-
ple all stood and began the

journey

back to their village, to the home of the boy

poet

who wrote the poem for the new Governor.

Everything Always

Sarah smiled sweetly.
The smile believers see on the face
of a loved one just before they pass over.
A knowing smile that promises
Everything, Always.

The other thirty-five people in the church smiled
too. They sang hymns, and they prayed, some spoke
in tongues. They were filled with expectation as the
pastor confidently took a copperhead from a
wooden box labeled serpent, and carefully passed it
to young Sarah.

Now everyone knows the copperhead is slower and
safer than the timberland rattler, rattlers can get
jumpy - they're too unpredictable for a novice.
But everyone also knows that venom is venom, and
faith is faith. So when Sarah accepted the serpent
she did so with respect and care. She'd seen it done
many times before, and even though she

had witnessed three snakebites in her young life,
she was confident. Papa told her there are two ways
you get bitten, one is poor snake handling, and the
other is insufficient faith. If the snake did get her,
she hoped it was from poor snake handling,
she dreaded having to carry the scar of insufficient
faith. The pastor told her to keep the serpent away
from her face. He said if you are going to get bit,
best it is on the hand. Sarah looked into the hideous
eyes of the serpent, the reptilian, repugnant, scale
covered unemotional eyes that never blink.

There isn't a trance-like state in the world to mask the fear she felt growing inside her. No amount of bible study or pastor's sermons prepared her for this moment – all she could do was pray. She silently recited the 23rd Psalm, because Psalms always calmed her in times of need. The Lord is my Shepherd; fear no evil, relief from my distress. As Sarah recited the Psalm the spirit of peace swept over her.

They say animals can sense fear, Papa told her their dog Butch could sense fear. That's why he bit the delivery man, but Sarah didn't believe that. Sarah believed she could fool an animal, she could fool the pastor, and she could fool a serpent, but no one can fool God. God knows what's in your heart. Jesus had said, those with sufficient faith will pick up snakes with their hands and it will not hurt them. She loved God with all her heart and she wondered if God would allow her to substitute love for faith? Sarah slowly lifted the serpent above her head. The pastor had told her to focus on the faces of her friends and family, to fill her heart with love. But there in the shadow of her two favorite cousins, the eyes of the man she had hoped never to see again, the man who rarely attended church, were staring intently at her. It was her uncle, the molester, who had messed with her around harvest time. She quickly looked away and trying to calm her mind with prayer and psalms, but all that came forth were bad thoughts. She wanted to scream. God, have mercy on me!

She wanted to drop the snake and run from the church, from the serpent, from her uncle. But as the venom of fear pumped through her veins and arteries Sarah knew it was futile to run. She couldn't outrun God. She could risk her parents' disapproval or the pastor's, but she couldn't risk eternal damnation. She couldn't risk Everything Always. She closed her eyes. Lord, help me please don't let it bite me! Please Lord, take this from me! Forsake me not! Please! When she opened her eyes her outstretched hands were empty, the serpent had vanished.

Sarah moved from the stage and sat between her proud parents. Her father put his deformed snake-bitten hand around her shoulder. Sarah watched the pastor carefully put the serpent back into the wooden box. She felt an odd attachment to the snake and she realized then that it wasn't the pastor that had chosen that snake. God had chosen the snake to be as a divine instrument so that faith would be manifest through her.

The Holy Spirit entered everyone in the room that day, and it entered the snake too. Sarah had stared into the eyes of the snake and didn't see God, but God through the eyes of the snake, had seen Sarah. God saw her fear and her imperfections, and God loved her still. As the pastor closed the lid of the wooden box, Sarah caught one final glimpse of the Chosen One. Sarah smiled sweetly. The smile of a 14-year-old girl who had just seen Everything Always.

Words Are Cheap, But I Have a Museum Quality Love

Words are cheap.

That's what she said to me.
I need you to show me that you care about me.
So after she went to work, because I obviously
lacked the gene required for emotional connection,
I made an effort to compensate by looking up
the word show in the dictionary.

To cause or allow to be seen, to display.

So I gathered together my best love poems
and wrote all day, until I had 100 poems.
Then I rushed through the apartment taping
the 100 poems to the walls of every room,
hurrying to finish before she arrived home.
And when she did enter the apartment it had
become an art gallery, the testament of my love.

In measured steps she walked silently from
room to room, stopping here and there,
to read a poem. In the kitchen,
she took an apple from a bowl on the counter,
and took a bite at the reddest point.
Then, when she had read several more poems,
she removed one from the wall and stuck it to my
shirt.

I like this one; it's museum quality,

she said, as she handed me the once-bitten apple.

I watched her walk down the hallway
towards the bedroom, along the way her clothes
falling off her body.

I found a pencil on the counter, and in the space
where she had removed the poem from the wall I
wrote,

Words Are Cheap, but I Have a Museum Quality
Love.

And then with the poem she had chosen still
hanging from my chest, and her once-bitten apple
in my hand,
I went straight to the bedroom.

One Dusty Book at a Time

There's a certain musty smell
that settles into used bookstores
in a range somewhere between
newspaper ink and Turkish coffee grounds
that I find appealing.

It's no secret that when it comes to books
I prefer paper over electronic submission,
and I have a particular soft spot in my heart
for the abandoned, books wedged into cardboard
boxes and left hurriedly at the proprietors' back
door, orphans forced into the book trades, and
subject to a life of degrading disclaimers.

The polite, Some shelf-wear, or Notes in the margins
(usually, Man versus Nature).
Dust jacket missing, which at that age
should go without saying. Then there is the
amusing, Corners dog-eared, and Foxed brown
spots, whatever they are.
And as you might expect, the embarrassing
designations, Damp stained, Loose binding, and
Worming. will have the most difficulty finding a
good home.

And I always feel sorry for the Ex-library copy,
who have spent a life shuttling from home to home.
The ones most people resent because they used
to be able to take them home without charge.
Among the hopeful you can find the Re-jointed,
just back from rehabilitation, sporting new stitches

or a repaired spine, they do look healthier.
And you probably won't be surprised to hear
that Autographed copy and First edition
get the best shelf space.

But I love them all the same, Like New, Good,
the Acceptable, paperbacks and hardcovers.
I want to cradle them all in my arms and remind
them that they still possess the magic to make
children laugh, fill our minds with hours of
adventure, spark our imaginations,
evoke tears and bring about smiles. They remind us
of the joy in the human experience, one dusty book
at a time.

I'm Not Here Right Now

The first time I heard her voice after she had died,
the hair on the back of my neck tingled,
a sure sign that the dead are about.
My sad eyes scanned the darkness of our house
searching for her, as if she was playfully hiding
behind a door, curtain or piece of furniture,
in one of the nearby room.

        I'm not here right now...

declared her disincarnate voice.
How can I mourn her loss when she answers
each call as if she has stepped out for groceries?

        Leave a message...

The ring and click of well-intended messages,
accumulating on the phone like dreary Buffalo
snow.
I could change the message, but I'm certain
she'd find other more severe ways to haunt me.

        I'm not here right now...

I'm not here right now either.
I'm hiking in the woods hand-in-hand with you.
We're dancing under the light of a Caribbean moon.
I'm shivering with you under a wet tropical water-
fall.
I'm tight up against you, warming myself
with the heat from the skin of your naked body

as we sleep upon each other like curled snakes,
dreaming the same dream, the dream where
the phone impersonates you and tells me

I'm not here right now...

The one sure thing I already know.

Moths

In the evening, after dinner, I take my coffee
to the porch to warm myself by the heat
lamp, and to count dead moths.

I'm curious why they chance such closeness
after the heat of the bulb
first singes their wispy wings.

I can't imagine being a creature that
flirts with its destiny that easily.
But when a lifespan is measured in days

rather than decades, who can find fault
with any creature emerging from
the dark woods to fix on a light

so overwhelmingly pleasing
that it's impossible to look away.
Why does behavior so inevitable,

simple, and mysterious evoke such
deep curiosity? Perhaps if my life-span
were numbered in days I would

devote less moments of my life
in contemplation of my role as
magi or executioner?

That's what I think each evening,
without fail, after dinner, when
I take my ritual walk to the front porch

to count scorched wings and place
my scarred cheek near the heat lamp,
a light that passes all understanding.

Good Reception

When I was a kid we owned a console television.
A big wooden cabinet that housed both a large
picture tube and a built in speaker.

The television set had a big clunky dial that clicked
when you rotated it to find one of three channel
options. And to make matters worse, it sometimes
came off in your hand.

But the most interesting component of the
television console was the rabbit ear antenna, the
two metal rods placed on top of the television to
facilitate good reception.

The challenge being to turn the antennae this way
and that or cross them over each other in the hope
of find that just right position that brought the
picture into focus.

But Dad knew of a trick. Wrap the antennae with
aluminum foil, because science tells us that
aluminum is an excellent conductor of the particle
waves that carry light and sound. The science

of which I admit to having little understanding. The
rabbit ears, and my dependence on them, are gone
now, but I meet a woman who has designed a rabbit
ear aluminum helmet,

a device she swears by. It's how she receives
instruction –

intentional artistic creativity. She says reception is best in the morning and late at night, but fades midday.

Sometimes I lend my experience, confidently moving her antennae until clearly through the static, I hear Dad's voice, *right there, don't move, hold it right there*!

Come Back to the War, Handsome Johnny

Hey, look yonder, tell me what you see
marching to the fields of Vietnam?
It looks like Handsome Johnny with an M15.
            Richie Havens & Lou Gossett

Come back to the war, Handsome Johnny.
There is no need for you to sit
in that plywood paneled basement,
starring at the empty walls, drinking
a blue ribbon beer, smoking a joint,
picking at your bleeding cuticles until
the pain reminds you that you're alive.
Come back to the war, Handsome Johnny.

Come back to the action, the excitement,
the adrenaline induced high of shadow soldiers
moving in the mist, the glint of gun metal,
strange words, and the click of a trigger in the
cold dead night, come back to your friends Johnny,
we know what you're feeling, we've got your back,
we're a team. We love you, man.
Come back to the war, Handsome Johnny.

Medical Horses

Straightaway

I want to know,

did Humpty Dumpty slip,

jump, or get pushed

from the wall,

and why were the King's

horses summoned?

The last thing I need is

a herd of medical horses

stomping around the crime scene

before the forensic team arrives.

Eye of the Beholder

The museum painting of two old men sitting
on an wooden bench under a chestnut tree
set me to wondering about them.
Alfredo and Rocco, who grew up together

in a small Italian village, playing football, cards,
and domino - doing what boys in small villages do.
Now old men with road map faces partially hidden

under wool hats that almost touch
as they lean in straining to hear each other's
stories of old friends and lovers,
children and grandchildren.

Tales embellished with each telling.
I imagined another painting where Alfredo,
the older of the two men by several months,
is standing in his kitchen, enjoying

the scent of garlic on his wife's hair,
and the taste of Chianti -
memories of communion -
now a remedy for his arthritis.

Telling his wife that the color of this barrel
of wine reminds him of a famous painting
he once saw in a gallery in Rome,
but he can't recall the painter.

That's what I saw as I stared in awe at the
painting of two old men sitting under a tree

sharing their love of life and liberty,
when the artist arrived to tell me that

he wasn't sure who the men in his painting
were, but he could tell me with certainty that
they weren't Italians, but two Armenia's
talking about the weather.

The Boston Tea Party

I imagine they weren't very convincing,
Sam Adams and the Sons of Liberty,
dressed up as Narragansett Indians
in the dead of winter, wool blankets
thrown over their heads, faces painted with
coal dust compliments of the local silversmith,
and of course plenty of tomahawks.
It's a shame no one documented how the Natives
felt about such foolishness.

But for the patriots' taxation without
representation was serious business, and New
Englanders from as far away as Maine came to
Boston to protest, 116 men boarded three ships at
midnight, and over the next nine hours emptied
340 chests of tea leaf into Boston Harbor,
the equivalent of 18,523,000 cups of tea.

The tea was the property of the East Indian Tea
Company, a London based operation that traded
goods to China in exchange for tea, cotton, salt, and
opium. The tea dumped into the harbor was tea
grown in China, 240 chests were Bohea or black tea
harvested from the Wuyi Mountains in the Chinese
province of Fujian. The remaining 100 chests of tea
consisted of Singlo, Congov, Hyson, and Souchong.

In the early morning, their hands and hair
smelling strongly of tea, the patriots returned
to their homes with the exception of a small group
who made their way to the Green Dragon Tavern,

where the proprietor was serving coffee flavored
with honey and cinnamon. And in the exuberance
of a job well done a patriot, his cup raised,
shouted Tea is for Tories! And in that moment
coffee became the preferred beverage of all patriots.

I Want to Be Anthologized

I want to be anthologized.
I want to see my name in black ink
on the content page of a Best Of collection,
wedged between professors that teach
poetry classes at universities, and slam poets
who memorize and deliver staggering
numbers of lines in perfect cadence.

I want to be anthologized.
In the company of men who
write about the pain of war,
and emotional disconnection.
I want to be anthologized.
In the company of women
who write with passion and
conviction about their daughters,
mothers, and grandmothers.

I want to be anthologized.
with movers and shakers
who set their poems to music
and showcase them in videos.
And when the poetry revolution
does get televised I want to be there
with the best of them.
I want a cameo, screen credits,
and a small royalty check.

I want to be anthologized
with poets who write list poems:
one - I want to be the first poem in the anthology.

two - I'll settle for somewhere in the middle
three - Ok I'll be go last. I don't mind last.

I just want to be anthologized.
Hell, I'll even cast lots with poets
who use profanity as a literary technique.
Fuck, just put me in the damn anthology

www.ingramcontent.com/pod-product-compliance
Lightning Source LLC
Chambersburg PA
CBHW031612040426
42452CB00006B/488